BRANDEIS, WEIZMANN
AND EINSTEIN:
FOUR DAYS IN CLEVELAND;
JUNE, 1921

BRANDEIS, WEIZMANN AND EINSTEIN:
FOUR DAYS IN CLEVELAND;
JUNE, 1921

Joel Z. Wagman

Library of Congress Control Number: 2020908409
ISBN: Hardcover   978-1-9845-7813-6
                   Softcover   978-1-9845-7812-9
                   eBook   978-1-9845-7811-2

Print information available on the last page.

Rev. date: 05/12/2020

To order additional copies of this book, contact:
Xlibris
1-888-795-4274
www.Xlibris.com
Orders@Xlibris.com
813422

CONTENTS

INTRODUCTION

What you are about to read, began as a "Letter to the Editor", in response to an article entitled "Churchill and Dr. Chaim Weizmann: Scientist, Zionist and Israeli Statesman", by Fred Glueckstein, which appeared in "Finest Hour: The Magazine of the Churchill International Society" (Number 170: Fall 2015). However, when my "Letter" was completed, it was too long to serve its original purpose, but too short to be a book. Thus, for the sake of genre classification, the following is a somewhat protracted, but perhaps, thought provoking Essay.

Initially, I was prompted to write the Letter, because regrettably, Glueckstein's article related only a selective part of the historical record, inception and dynamic, of the problematic and complicated growth of Zionism. Moreover, Glueckstein submits to the exclusion of innumerable other relative factors, solely, the well-worn British-Zionist-Weizmann version of facts, regarding the extensive international efforts to convert Theodore Herzl's "Dream" of a Jewish State, into hard reality. ("Judenstadt: 1896"). Nonetheless, the course of history evidences that both prior and contemporary with British involvement in the Zionist saga, there were two other influential national Zionist proponents: namely: the Wilhelmine German Empire, and the United States of America. Without their respective essential contributions not only of extensive funding, but as well, early political commitment to the Zionist cause, during the close of the nineteenth century and the first two decades of the twentieth; Herzl's nascent, astonishing "Dream", never would have achieved its political fulfillment.

This, Essay, entitled "Brandeis, Weizmann, and Einstein: Four Days in Cleveland: June, 1921", is therefore the long-delayed response, to Gluekstein's original "Finest Hour" article. Its content seeks to redress what this writer perceives as overlooked omissions from the historic record, by shining a wider, brighter, illumination upon the irrefutable facts regarding the complicated birth of Israel. Facts, which through inadvertence, political prejudice – or both, were consigned a century ago to the dustbin of history. As subsequently shall be demonstrated, calculated decisive actions by the Weizmann-led "European" Zionist faction, were specifically designed to wrest control of World Zionism from Louis Brandeis and his associates of the American Zionist Organization; crystallizing with lamentable results in early June, 1921, during a crucial, few days in Cleveland, Ohio, which consequently, irrevocably changed the course of history.

DEDICATION

This Essay is dedicated to the memory of Sir Winston Churchill, without whose tireless, inspiring, efforts, in the direst of times and circumstances, there would be neither democracy, nor the State of Israel.

April 11, 2020

On February 14, 1949, Chaim Weitzmann was elected Israel's first President. In 1951, the long-standing stalwart friend of the Jewish people ,advocate of Israel and former and present British Prime Minister, Winston Churchill wrote to Weitzmann:

" The wonderful exertions which Israel is making in these times of difficulty are cheering to an old Zionist like me.I trust you may work with Jordan and the rest of the Muslim world. With true comradeship there will be room for all.

BRANDEIS, WEIZMANN AND EINSTEIN: FOUR DAYS IN CLEVELAND; JUNE, 1921

Zionism's purpose is, was, and remains to inculcate, prosper, maintain, and defend the Jewish peoples' historic and inalienable right to a nation situate on the ancestral lands of their ancient forebearers. Zionism is the infinite renewal of the blossoming of Herzl's dream of a 'Jewish National Homeland', in order to preserve and perpetuate the State of Israel. Herzl's unrelenting dream, of a reborn Jewish nation, after the passage of two millennia since the Roman conquest of Judea; the destruction of Solomon's Temple; the burning of Jerusalem, and the incalculable suffering and murder of millions of Jews; before, during and after the catastrophic Shoah, became manifest on May, 14, 1948.

That seminal date, was carefully timed to coincide with the expiry of the British Government's redundant and by 1948, totally meaningless, League of Nations Mandate. The League's Mandate, arose from the underlying Versailles Treaty (1919), primarily focusing and dealing with post-war Europe, which inadequately, replaced a thousand years of civilization with the American President Wilson's "Fourteen Points", national self-determination and vengeful monetary, territorial, and material reparations to be paid by Germany to the victorious Allied powers. Into that malignant stew stemmed the San Remo Treaty (1920), pertaining to the former Ottoman Empire Middle East territories. More importantly, the San Remo Treaty provided international recognition of the Balfour Declaration and its promise of a Jewish Homeland, as well as Arab minority rights within those territories. Thereby, deplorably creating a venomous relationship between Arab and Jew, which yet persists. An insignificant part of those Ottoman territories was unofficially referred to by European scholars and religious figures, as 'Palestine' (or 'South Syria'). But, officially, for both geographic and political purposes, for centuries had been known to the Ottomans as the 'Sanjak of Jerusalem'.

'If you will it; it is no dream', are the closing words of Herzl's novel "Altneuland" (1902). In certitude, within the relatively brief span from its 1895 commencement until 1914, Herzl's dream rapidly matured into a significant world-wide movement, ensuring that a Jewish State no longer was mere fantasy, but, assuredly, an attainable political reality. On that long anticipated day, at the Tel Aviv Museum in an overly hot room, crowded with 250 persons – upon an almost barren table, notably placed directly beneath the watchful eyes of Theodore Herzl's portrait – the members of the "Peoples' Council", gladly executed the "Declaration of The Establishment of the State of Israel".

What had ended in a Tel Aviv museum, during the early evening hours of May, 14, 1948, with an emotional Declaration read by David Ben Gurion establishing a Jewish State, began in 1895 in the recesses of Herzl's ever-creative mind, while he sat in his fashionable 'fin de siècle' Vienna apartment housing him, his wife and their two young children. Herzl's thoughts composed the geneses of what soon became contemporary secular Zionism: an inextinguishable idea, whose time, after over two millennia of patience and prayer finally had arrived. Within 53 years from Herzl's initial Vienna musings, there would be a Jewish nation: albeit a nation, with deep Germanic roots. For without the extensive German-Jewish support of Herzl's "Dream" and the resultant international Zionist movement (initially headquartered in Berlin); the future State of Israel probably would have been still-born as an early casualty of the tumultuous opening years of the Great War.

THEODORE HERZL: VISIONARY

" A Hungarian born, totally assimilated Jewish playwright, journalist and literary critic, who spoke neither Hebrew nor Yiddish, put up Christmas trees in his home, and did not bother to circumcise his son. Herzl was not much of a Jew", but enough of one to react to a new kind of political anti-Semitism erupting in the 1890's across Western Europe. That political, social and economic self-serving hatred of Jews was patent by Russia's continuing and ever-more vicious Pogroms; the overwhelming election as Mayor of Vienna of a virulent anti-Semitic demagogue named Karl Luegar, and the invidious French political-military cause-celebre, the notorious Dreyfus Affair.

Within those volatile, highly charged, public matters, the strikingly handsome, urbane Herzl rediscovered his long dormant sense of Jewishness. Tall, bearded, elegant in manner and speech, and unfailingly sartorially impeccable in wing-collar, ascot and frockcoat; Herzl was an integral part of the late nineteenth century's western and central European world of "Belle Lettre". It is undebatable, that in thought, opinion, philosophy and life style, Theodor Herzl was far more Austro-German, than Jewish.

Nevertheless, Herzl's reportage in Paris on behalf of the leading Viennese newspaper – 'Neue Freie Presse' respecting the condemnation, trial and expulsion from the French army, of Captain Alfred Dreyfus, and the accompanying febrile anti-Semitism of the Parisian mob, doubtlessly weighed heavily upon him

For, if Dreyfus, a totally assimilated French Jew – who, at the time, was nothing less than a member of the inner-circle intelligence section of the French Army's General Staff – could be wrongfully persecuted – then, what of Herzl – a so-called, Austrian? That overarching factor – whether conscious or otherwise, unmistakably influenced the creation of Herzl's eventual Dream. As to what would constitute the cultural and philosophical elements, of a newly created Jewish state – those ideas often expressed in excruciating detail, were wholly conjured in Herzl's fertile imagination.

The description in Simon Sebag Montefiore's, epic "Jerusalem: The Biography" (2011)", captures the full panoply and sense of the naive paradox, which constituted Herzl's embryonic vision of a Jewish state.

"..... At first, this half-pragmatist, half-utopian – dreamed of a German aristocratic republic, a Jewish Venice ruled by a senate with a Rothschild as a princely Doge and himself as Chancellor. His vision was secular: the high priest 'will wear impressive robes'; the Herzl army would boast cuirassiers with silver breast plates; his modern Jewish citizens would play cricket and tennis in a modern Jerusalem"

Herzl's ideal of a Germanified Jewish nation is synthesized by Geoffrey Wheatcroft in his "The Controversy of Zion" (1996), which further amplifies Herzl's naive vision.

"By that standard (general European colonization in the 1890's in Africa and Asia); there was nothing uniquely odd in Herzl's dream of transplanting the culture of the central European Jewish bourgeoisie to the Levant down to the most comical and touching detail. 'I shall transport over there, genuine Viennese cafes. With these small expedients, I shall ensure the desirable illusion of the old environment'.

He also believed that German would be the official language of the Jewish state but 'I have nothing, however, against French or English. I shall incline towards English sports, and in this way prepare them for the army. Along with cafes, football and cricket, Herzl wanted to transport the very idea of Europe to the Levant, just as the Crusaders had"

THE JEWISH STATE: A GERMAN PROTECTORATE?

The pragmatics of Herzl's newly-found "national will" was to be crystallized in the palaces and drawing rooms of Western Europe, and in particular, the court of the Imperial German monarch, Wilhelm II. It was Herzl's fundamental understanding of the layered structure of the Kaiser's obtuse personality, and the German Emperor's underlying sense of historic grandeur that not only birthed Zionism's early romance with Imperial Germany, but additionally led to the intertwining of early Zionism's need for a pacific and enduring relationship with the Ottomans.

It is therefore unsurprising that the major thrust of Herzl's objective in the establishment of a Jewish state was directed to the Kaiser. In doing so, Herzl was keenly aware that German political, economic and military aims included not only influencing the dynamic of Turkey's newly kindled nationalism, but that the extensive Ottoman Middle East territories afforded an unexcelled opportunity to thwart the future Near East ambitions of the Kaiser's English cousins. It was to this rising Imperial German star that Herzl decided to hitch the ascending Zionist wagon.

"I shall go to the German Kaiser (to say), "Let our people go", decided Herzl, and resolved to base his new state on "this great, strong, moral, splendidly governed, tightly organized Germany. Through Zionism it will become possible for Jews to love this Germany."

To convert his plan for a Zionist-Imperial German alliance into palpable reality, Herzl had to penetrate the Kaiser's court. "First, he managed to meet, the Kaiser's influential uncle, the Grand Duke Friedrich of Baden, who was interested in a scheme to find the Ark of the Covenant. Baden wrote to his nephew, who in turn asked Philip, Prince of Eulenburg to report on the Zionist plan. Eulenburg – the Kaiser's best friend, ambassador to Vienna and political mastermind, was 'fascinated' by Herzl's advocacy. Zionism was a clear opportunity to extend the reach of German influence and power. The Kaiser agreed that "the energy creativity and efficiency of the tribe of Shem would be diverted to worthier goals than the sucking dry of Christians". Despite the Kaiser's obvious social (if not yet political) anti-Semitism, Herzl received glad tidings when His Imperial Majesty paradoxically acknowledged "Everywhere the hydra of the ghastliest anti-Semitism is raising its dreadful head and the terrified Jews are looking around for a protector. Well then, I will intercede with the Sultan". Herzl was ecstatic; to be sure, his diary for that day records of the meeting; "Wonderful, wonderful."

On 11 October 1898, the Kaiser and Kaiserin together with an appropriately large retinue departed for Jerusalem. Herzl and four Zionist colleagues were closely behind, as they left Vienna for the same destination via the Orient Express on October, 13. "In Istanbul (then Constantinople), the Kaiser deigned to receive the Zionists. The Kaiser inquired what he should ask the Sultan for. 'A chartered company under German protection' replied Herzl: Whereupon, the Kaiser invited Herzl to meet him in Jerusalem.

"On 2 November, Herzl was summoned for his Imperial audience", which occurred at the Kaiser's ultra-luxurious grand encampment just north of Jerusalem's Damascus Gate "Herzl found the Kaiser posing in a grey colonial uniform, brown gloves, veiled helmet and holding (oddly enough) a riding crop. The Zionist delegation (clad in formal white tie, black tails and top hats), approached, halted and bowed. Wilhelm held out his hand very affably to Herzl and commenced to lecture him. The land needs water and shade. There is room for all. The idea behind your movement is a healthy one".

In the event, Wilhelm proposed the Zionist plan to the Ottoman Sultan Abdul-Hamid, who firmly, and utterly rejected it – telling his daughter – prophetically "The Jews may spare their millions: when my empire is divided, perhaps they will get Palestine for nothing. But only our corpse can be divided". Nevertheless, that seeming finality was not the end of German-Zionist Holy Land involvement or of German plans for a future protectorate over a Zionist Middle East state.

Granting the incontestable fact that from its earliest days there was a deeply seated German connection to Zionism; the question is therefore begged; how did the British (the promulgators of the 1917 Balfour Declaration and its inherent avowal of a "Jewish Homeland"), become involved in the murky, deep, Ottoman waters of the Middle East? For that answer we must turn to the definitive "A Peace to End All Peace" by David Fromkin (1989), who posits.

"When Herzl, an assimilated Jew, conceived the idea of political Zionism" his notion was that Jews needed a national homeland – but its location was not of primary importance. "Of Jews and Judaism, Herzl knew next to nothing. He was a fashionable journalist, the Paris correspondent of a Viennese newspaper, who had all but forgotten his Jewish origins, until the shock of French anti-Semitism flowing unabated from the Dreyfus case convinced him of the need to rescue the world's Jews from their historical plight.

"As a man of the world he knew how political business was transacted in the Europe of his time, and began establishing a Zionist organization." He then commenced negotiations on its behalf, with several governments. It was only after coming into contact with other Jews and organizations of a like mind, which for years had been establishing and fostering Jewish settlements in the Holy Land that Herzl came to realize the singularity of "the country that the world called Palestine – the Land of the Philistines—but the Jews called the Land of Israel".

At the advent of the twentieth century, Herzl's discussions with Ottomans had persuaded him that the Sultan was loath to agree to any Zionist proposal relevant to Palestine, and that he should look elsewhere for fulfillment. "In 1902 Herzl held an important discussion with Joseph Chamberlain, the father of British Imperialism and authoritative Colonial Secretary of both the Salisbury and Balfour Cabinets. Chamberlain, too, believed in a national solution for the Jewish problem". He therefore listened carefully to Herzl's several alternatives regarding Palestine, which, in the result, focused on the feasibility of Jewish settlements in nearby Egyptian (British controlled), territory.

This, however, was to be a temporary measure, made in the fond hope that somehow – in some way – Palestine eventually would become accessible to Zionist immigration. As shortly will be seen, this proposal was but an early foray by the British into the arcane territories of the Ottoman Middle East.

Within a few years, the British Government in combination with the British Zionist movement ultimately would prove to be an unbeatable duo. In the meantime, the Germans and their indigenous Zionists, to all appearances, were still 'Top-Dogs' in the future disposition of the Holy Land conundrum.

GERMANY, THE OTTOMANS, ZIONISM AND THE ARRIVAL OF THE GREAT WAR

At the dawn of the cataclysmic Great War, the offices of the Zionist World Organization ("ZWO") were located at 8 Sachsische Strasse, Berlin. As was the case with many other international organizations, the ZWO's cosmopolitan executive committee of two Germans, one Austrian and three Russians, was ill-prepared for the outbreak of a World War. It resulted in divided and clashing loyalties – not only among the executive of the Zionist World Congress, but in its world-wide diverse membership. In "A History of Zionism" (1972), its distinguished author Walter Lacquer writes.

"That the world movement was to stay out of the conflict and remain neutral goes without saying, but this was easier said than done. For the Zionist leaders throughout Europe, with the obvious exception of Russia, felt it their duty, to support their respective fatherlands to the best of their ability. This conflict of loyalties apart, there was the question of protecting Palestinian Jewry. Above all, there was the issue of the postwar settlement. Some Zionist leaders realized early on that what their movement had failed to attain in time of peace, it might well achieve during or after a war, which was bound to lead to a re-examination of many unresolved international issues": including that of an incipient Zionist Palestine. It was only a question of time and which nation (or group of nations), the Zionist leaders would choose as Zionism's major ally.

As has been earlier averred, there were three major contenders for the affections of Zionism: The Imperial Germans, the United States of America, and the British Empire. The relationships among the Allies, the central powers and world Zionism, as well, was no simple matter; but, indeed, complex and fraught with extreme political difficulty; not only because of the clashing ambitions of the national competitors; but additionally, because of its unaddressed, inevitable, consequences upon world Jewry.

As Lacquer succinctly declares in defining the national competitors "The patriotic enthusiasm of the German and Austrian Zionists seems in retrospect singularly misguided, but it is only fair to add that the war against Russia was equally popular, in Eastern Europe and the United States, the two biggest Jewish concentrations. The fact that after the outbreak of war, the persecution of Jews in western Russia became even more intense, and that hundreds of thousands of them had been deported, did not make that country any more popular. Most leaders of Russian and Polish Jewry believed in the inevitability of a German victory. For them, as Weizmann once opined," the West ended at the Rhine". A Russian victory would perpetuate the persecution of east European Jewry, whereas the defeat of Russia was bound to open the gates of their liberation. By allying themselves with Russia – France and Britain – Zionism had become its knowing accessories in crime" . . . the greater part of the world Zionist movement was pro-German, even though it became more reserved after the first flush of excitement. Historical sympathies and antipathies apart, a strong case could be made for the continuing importance of Berlin to Zionists.

Effective political and economic aid to the hard-pressed Palestinian Jewish community could be extended only from the German capital during the first three years of the War. During this time, the German Armies advanced far into western Russia and the bulk of Polish and Lithuanian Jewry came under German rule. Whichever way one looked at it, as far as Zionist politics were concerned – Berlin was both the focus and pivot.

According to Sebag Montefiore, it was the same story in Palestine." When the commander of the Ottoman troops in Palestine – the Bavarian General, Kress von Kressenstein arrived, the Jews of Jerusalem welcomed his units, with a triumphal arch. The Germans had now assumed protection of the Jews from the British"

ENTER THE
UNITED STATES

Notwithstanding, the deep-rooted German-Zionist involvement, in addition to the British, there was one other nation incisively involved: The United States of America. Due to Wilson's 1912 election as President, and his appointment of Henry Morgenthau Sr. as American Ambassador to the Ottomans; the Balfour Declaration would have been nothing more than a lonely good intention, and the State of Israel a dead, forgotten dream buried in the sands of Ottoman Arabia

In early August, 1913 after strenuous pressure from his colleagues, co-religionists and family, Henry Morgenthau Senior, financier, entrepreneur, humanitarian and visionary, whatever his reluctance, consented to accept President Wilson's offer to be the American Ambassador to the Ottoman Empire. It was not – in the least – what he wanted. Indeed, after being the chief financial architect of the Democrat Party in the Election of November, 1912, making possible the elevation of Woodrow Wilson to the Presidency; Morgenthau fully and fairly anticipated becoming the first Democrat of the Jewish faith to achieve Cabinet status. Nevertheless, Wilson had other, more substantial plans, for him.

Thus, began, a series of meetings between Wilson and Morgenthau, which stretched over several months concerning American Mideast policy and Morgenthau's ambassadorship to the "Porte". The new

American Middle East foreign policy as promulgated by Wilson was made crystalline clear, when the President said to Morgenthau:

"Constantinople is the point at which the interests of American Jews and the welfare of Jews of Palestine are focused; it is almost indispensable that I have a Jew at that post".

In September, 1913, Morgenthau's nomination received the unanimous approval of the U.S. Senate. At their farewell conference, Wilson with sincerity, warmth and affection, said to the newly minted Ambassador: "remember that anything you can do to improve the lot of your co-religionists is an act that will reflect upon America, and you may count on the full power of this Administration to back you up"

Morgenthau and the ambassadorial party embarked for their exotic destination on the appropriately named liner 'George Washington'. While on board he met several highly placed Protestant medical and educational missionaries, who were en route to their posts in the Holy Land. Several months later in pursuance to his instructions from Wilson, Morgenthau visited Palestine on a fact-finding mission; where he was reunited with several of those whom he had first encountered on the George Washington.

(As shall be subsequently discussed, less than a year after his visit, Morgenthau was to receive numerous reports from the American missionary community, as to the thinly-disguised hostility of the "Young Turk" Ottoman administration toward both Christians and Jews).

Soon after Ambassador Morgenthau's arrival in the Ottoman capital, the aggressive, highly nationalist and recently installed 'Young Turk' government, placed severe restrictions on further Jewish (mainly Russian in national origin) immigration, including: the introduction of a so-called Red Card, which grudgingly permitted a stay in Palestine of only three months.

Morgenthau, German born and an American success story, was not a Zionist: far from it: holding to his last breath anti-Zionist opinions and sentiments. Undeniably, however he was also proudly Jewish. Morgenthau, well-remembering Wilson's strict admonition at the time of their farewell meeting, became increasingly troubled by recurring thoughts of probable Turkish retribution upon Palestine's hapless Jews. Thoroughly distrusting all Turkish protestations to the contrary, and realizing full-well that the temper of the times would only make matters worse; prior to returning to Constantinople from the Holy Land, he submitted a request to several of the Protestant missionaries to inform him immediately concerning any overt or rumored change in Ottoman administrative or political policies, which, even remotely, could negatively affect his Jewish brethren.

At month's end, April, 1914, Morgenthau resumed his duties in the Ottoman capital. Within ninety days, the grisly specter of war ever more stalked the Near and Middle East. With the inevitable commencement of hostilities in early August in Western Europe and Russia, Morgenthau realized that his obligations entailed much more than anyone originally had contemplated, when he reluctantly accepted Wilson's challenge to be America's chief envoy to the Ottomans.

Morgenthau's granddaughter – the famed historian – Barbara Tuchman, in an article published in the May,1977, edition of Commentary Magazine', provides a touching summary of the extremely harsh—if not impossible – circumstances, pertaining in Palestine during 1914. A condition and plight, with which, both Morgenthau in Constantinople, and the Holy Land Jews had to closely contend.

"About half the Jewish population in Palestine including many of the older group and most of the new colonists were Russian by nationality, and had preferred to remain stateless rather than become Ottoman subjects. Consequently, they were now subject to treatment by the Turks as enemy aliens, with no recourse to protection by Russia, whose Pogroms they had fled. Expulsion and even massacres became imminent threats, impelling the American Ambassador to take not only increasing efforts to mitigate the harsh measures of the Turks – but, concurrently activating, the aid of the American and Allied governments" Morgenthau knew it would be up to him to ensure that no harm befell his fellow Jews; whether they were Zionist, or not; whether they were secular or religious.

Less than two weeks before the November, 2, 1914 entry of the Ottomans into World War One, Morgenthau received a letter couched in obtuse language, from Dr. Arthur Ruppin, who operated Zionist activities in Palestine; that Djemal – the Ottoman Generalissimo of Syria-Palestine, had been 'instructed to proceed against the Jews with great vigor and that he should immediately hinder their work'. When Morgenthau contacted Washington as to what he should do; Morgenthau's instructions received from William Jennings Bryan, the U.S. Secretary of State were precise and unequivocal, "exercise your best judgment consistent with American ideals."

It soon became progressively evident that while a 'final solution' was already underway against the Armenians, the Turks planned a similar fate for Palestine's Jews. Included in their agenda was the immediate implementation of 'financial strangulation', as witnessed by the Turk's recent and capricious closing of the Anglo-Palestine Bank. For the Jewish community heavily dependent on outside aid, the inevitable result, unless funds were soon forthcoming – would be eventual death by starvation. Finally, there was the heartless pillaging of livestock and grain leveled against the region's entire civilian population to supplement Turkish military requirements.

In response, Morgenthau devised a bold, imaginative and efficient plan consisting of money and logistics. Taking advantage of America's neutrality, Morgenthau's plan directed financial assistance to be channeled to American residents and corporations in the Near East, to enable them to purchase sufficient quantities of food and water, to ensure the survival of Palestine's Jews. And, moreover, to transfer by means of American ships, thousands of Jews to relatively near-by (British controlled) Egyptian ports, where they would be provided compassionate refuge for the remainder of the war.

To accomplish that solely humanitarian purpose, German co-operation would be imperative. To carry his audacious plan to fruition, Morgenthau intended to enlist the German Ambassador to the Ottomans—von Wagenheim, the German-Jewish-American financial establishment, German Zionist and non-Zionist organizations, various German foreign and economic ministries, and if necessary, the German Emperor himself. In "Mostly Morgenthaus: A Family History" (1991) its author, Henry Morgenthau III sheds clarification.

On August, 28, 1914, Morgenthau cabled Jacob Schiff the highly influential head of the German-American banking house Kuhn-Loeb, and Chairman of the Jewish American Committee:

"Palestine Jews facing terrible crises, belligerent countries stopping their assistance. Serious destruction threatens thriving colonies. Fifty thousand dollars needed by responsible committee"

Contemporaneously, Ambassador Morgenthau not only arranged with Standard Oil to have the $50,000 in American cash (presently about $900,000) converted into gold specie and released through Standard's representative in Constantinople. But, additionally, gained the unlimited support and co-operation, regarding the provision of U.S. warships to carry the gold and transfer the Jewish émigrés to Egypt from: President Woodrow Wilson, Secretary of State, William Jennings Bryan, and Josephus Daniels, Secretary of the Navy.

In an address to The American Historical Association in December, 1976 published in Commentary as "The Assimilationist Dilemma: Ambassador Morgenthau's Story" (May, 1977). Barbara Tuchman gave her version of the events touching upon Ambassador Morgenthau's cable (as a young child Tuchman was present in Constantinople during the summer of 1914 with her mother Alma Morgenthau, and her father Maurice Wertheim, while the momentous events occurred).

The non-Zionist "Henry Morgenthau Sr., in one of history's classic ironies . . . by his alert dispatch of assistance to the Zionist colonies in Palestine during August,1914 – while serving as the American Ambassador to Turkey . . . saved them from starvation and probable extinction, thus preserving the Jewish colonists for ultimate statehood".

"Speaking at a meeting in March, 1916, hosted by Felix Warburg (the German-American-Jewish banker): one of the foremost American Zionist leaders (and first president and chancellor of Hebrew University), Judah Magnes said of Morgenthau's critical intervention 'no word can be too strong, no expression too exaggerated' to describe the historical task thus performed"

In September, 1914, the USS North Carolina, her sister ship USS Tennessee, Maurice Wertheim and other Americans— Jews and non-Jews alike – all played transcendental roles in the drama of the miraculous survival of Palestine's Jewry. Absent the support of Bryan, Daniels, and Wilson, together with the U.S. Navy ships, it is highly doubtful that the $50,000 in gold specie would have reached its Haifa destination (and, even more importantly, the transfers of further extensive, vital, funds, which soon followed).

Spearheaded by Morgenthau and ably assisted by members of the American Jewish Committee (led by Schiff, in co-ordination with his German Zionists associates and their American political allies); the American Ambassador, was able to affect the rescue of Palestine's Jews from starvation. Those many admirable, unsung persons were the bellwether of the future: for without their prodigious efforts – now seemingly lost in the cauldron of more convenient political legends and myths; there would have been too few, or far worse, no Jews alive at all in Palestine – during November, 1917. Thereby, rendering redundant, obsolete, and unnecessary, the letter from the British Cabinet to Lord Walter Rothschild that His Majesty's Government favored the establishment of a Jewish Homeland within the borders of post-war, Palestine.

In 1917, the bulk of American Jews cheered and prayed for a German victory. In that soulful wish they were as one with their co-religionists not only in Germany but, as well, throughout Central and Eastern Europe. The results were demonstrated in the co-operation of Germany in expediting substantial funds to the threatened Palestinian Jews. As Lacquer provides in his "History of Zionism" "Effective political and economic aid to the hard-pressed Palestinian Jewish community could only be extended from the German capital during the first three years of the war. That telling statement is consistent with Henry Morgenthau III's, in Mostly Morgenthaus, wherein he states, 'with much of the funding channeled through German banks.

Morgenthau, Schiff, and the other constituents of the American Jewish Committee by prudency alone had to be aware that the initial $50,000 was woefully inadequate to serve the needs of the Yishuv (the indigenous Jewish population of Palestine). To successfully fulfill that objective a far greater amount obviously was required, enough, in fact, to last the duration of the war, Since no one knew when that happy day would occur, a pattern of procedural conduct and precedent relative to on-going future transfer of German originated funds to Palestine's Jews fortuitously was expeditiously established.

No matter what its amount or where emanated, those unascertained funds could arrive in Constantinople and thence to Palestine, only by means of the unimpaired resources of the German Zionist Organization, subject to the consent of the German government.

Such state of affairs is plainly acknowledged in "Mostly Morgenthaus"

"Later there would be far larger sums and other U.S. ships would bring in essential supplies, and carry harassed, frightened, sick and weary refugees out to safety . . . . The American mission was supported not without complication by the allied powers with much of the funding channeled through German banks even when the war was on (between the U.S. and Germany, aided by the Schiff-Warburg (banking) connections"

The British government took these developments very seriously. Amos Elon in his book "the Pity of it all" (2002), states: In a fit of paranoia the British Ambassador to Washington, even suspected the existence of a veritable German-Jewish conspiracy in the United States directed at Britain. Causing Arthur Balfour, the former Prime Minister and presently the Foreign Secretary of Great Britain, to proceed in haste to Washington. While there, he discussed with Wilson and his chief advisor relative to such matters – Louis Brandeis – a draft of the letter to Lord Rothschild, which later became known as the 'Balfour Declaration.' In the event, changes to the draft Declaration as suggested by Brandeis, were, in fact, made.

The 1917 Declaration in part was motivated by "the British government's desire to win support among pro-German American Jews ". To which, can be added that British intelligence sources, had also confirmed to the Cabinet, that a German version regarding a Jewish State or Homeland, was almost ready to be declared. The focal point of the events transpiring centered on the distinguished personage of Louis D. Brandeis, who on June 1, 1916, deservedly became Mr. Justice Brandeis of the Supreme Court of the United States.

LOUIS BRANDEIS: ZIONISM'S ALMOST FORGOTTEN HERO

Brandeis provided the overarching nexus between the Non-Zionist, generally pro-German, American Jewish Committee, and the nascent but growing American Zionist movement. Until he was 56 years of age, Brandeis had little to do with Judaism – let alone Zionism. Nonetheless, he evolved into one of the most important – and, for a time, the most significant of all world Zionist leaders. Between 1912, when he first appeared on a Zionist platform: and, 1921, when Weizmann engineered his tactless and brutal ejection from both the American and world Zionist movements. Brandeis activities and efforts on behalf of all the diverse concomitants of global Jewry, were, remain, and endure, in retrospect – totally unselfish, utterly constructive and incisively visionary as to the future of a Jewish nation.

As stated in Lacquer's "History of Zionism".

"Brandeis was almost 60 when he undertook his new role as a Jewish statesman." Above all, he never failed to emphasize that he had come to Zionism, not only late, but wholly as an American, who saw himself as a better American because he wanted a homeland for his people.

Brandeis, contemporaneously was both a figure of national prominence, and a leading voice of the American Zionist movement. "An eminently successful and popular lawyer, a friend and confidant of politicians, he was in line for a leading position", in Wilson's first administration of 1913.

Brandeis, however, the "people's attorney, had made many enemies among the rich", who still harbored anti-Semitic feelings – even against Brandeis – a gracious and noble Jew. Wilson, in consequence, nominated Brandeis for the Supreme Court. After the nomination was approved, Wilson wrote to Morgenthau, informing him that he "never signed any commission with such satisfaction".

Brandeis prestige, and his reputation as one of President Wilson's closest advisors, was an asset of which 'full use was made by Zionist leaders in London in their dealings with the British government'. London closely followed developments on the American domestic scene. Its sole aim being to induce America to join the war against the central powers as soon as possible.

The British were aware that while most of the leaders of American Jewry were pro-British (with few exceptions), the Jewish masses were decidedly anti-Russian and welcomed Russian defeats, while not necessarily rejoicing at German victories.

A change, in this respect, began to appear during 1916-17. The influential Jews of German descent were antagonized by such events as the ruthless 1915 sinking of the Lusitania. Whereas, the immigrants from Eastern Europe were finally being won over to the Allies by the advent of the Russian revolution of March, 1917 – which, belatedly, gave equal rights to Russian Jewry.

Paducah Kentucky, born and bred, Brandeis was as patrician an American Jew, as America's Eastern European immigrants, were essentially, still Europeans: Not yet ready to either accept or fully commit to the promise of their new-found "golden America". It was Brandeis that reconciled the widely divergent views as to the meaning of Zionism, by clearly defining that Zionism did not necessarily imply abandoning one's traditional homeland in favour of immigrating to a Jewish state promised, actual or otherwise. That simple proposition embracing the greater part of world Jewry distinguished the Zionist movement's shades of complexity, whereby indigenous Jewish national assimilation no longer was incompatible with the Zionist ideal, of a return to the Holy Land (that is to say; making 'Aliyah': literally an "ascent").

In his position as the embodiment of worldwide Zionism, the American educated Brandeis possessed both the birthright and fundamental credentials to provide American Zionism with the gravitas that previously had escaped it. In the nine years from 1912 to 1921, when he lost the struggle with Weizmann regarding whose vision of the future Jewish state would be dominant; Brandeis accomplished for Zionism what no other person saves perhaps – even, Weizmann had or would possess, until 1948. That accomplishment particularly was applicable during the period of America's World War One neutrality, when Brandeis co-ordinated Zionist activity in Berlin with other world capitals, giving credence to the truth of Lacquer's unqualified words, "aid to the Palestinian Jewish community could be extended only from the German capital during the first three years of the war".

Before 1914 concluded, in order to preserve its official neutrality, the World Zionist Organization, was relocated from Berlin to New York City. From its new Manhattan headquarters, Brandeis and his colleagues exerting considerable influence with Wilson became the essential link between the European (notably Austro-German) Zionists, American Zionists, and the non-Zionist American Jewish Committee.

With Brandeis at the helm, the World Zionist Provisional Committee, as Lacquer states; "helped to co-ordinate the rescue efforts for Palestinian Jewry, which cut off from Europe was facing economic ruin, Jews by unwritten tradition, such as: Morgenthau and Elkus, his successor in Constantinople, played a role second only to the Germans as the protector of the Yishuv (the Jewish population of Palestine) . . . . They intervened countless times with the Porte against the deportation orders issued in Jerusalem and Jaffa."

It was this improbable, combination of widely diverse opinions and objectives, which from August, 1914 until September, 1917, narrowly averted the Ottoman eradication of Palestine's Jewry. As history amply demonstrates, that unparalleled international combination of forces and personalities, began with Morgenthau's' cable to Schiff, and the humane mission of the American armored cruisers the Tennessee and

North Carolina. Without them, and persons such as Brandeis, there would not have been a State of Israel: there would not have been a Balfour Declaration: and, in all certainty, there would have been few, if any, Jews whatever in their ancient Holy Land. "By these measures, the nucleus of the future state of Israel survived".

In her 1976 address, to the American Historical Society, Barbara Tuchman offers "another contribution to the future of Israel, as important in a different way, was the support that made possible the revival of Hebrew, as a living language. Eliazar Ben Yehuda, the compiler – one, might say, the creator, of the Modern Hebrew dictionary, was brought to this country (the U.S.) in 1914 under Zionist auspices to continue his work in safety during the war years. But, the funds to support him and his family while he worked, as well as a house to live in and schooling for his daughters, were arranged for by my father (Maurice Wertheim), who had visited Ben Yehuda in Jerusalem, and paid for by my grandfather Jacob Wertheim and a committee consisting of Jacob Schiff, Felix Warburg, Julius Rosenwald and Herbert Lehman, the magnates of the so-called golden ghetto": all of them – without exception – non-Zionists. Thus, in the comfort and grace of a German American-Jewish environment in Chicago, was born the national language of Israel. [1]

BRANDEIS AND WEIZMANN: THE OLD-WORLD VERSUS THE NEW; THE STRUGGLE FOR LEADERSHIP OF ZIONISM: PINSK AGAINST PADUCAH

What, then, occurred as between the American Zionists headed by Brandeis and those Zionists in Great Britain, which led to a prolonged schism within the Zionist ranks: A fracture, of such serious proportion, that it yet bears undetermined consequence? The schism or rather the search for recognition of an American brand of Zionism which began in 1920 – continued until the late 1930's: when Hitlerism, forced Zionist ranks to close. To be sure, that schism, albeit in modified form may still exist politically, not only in the Diaspora, but in Israel itself – waiting for history to repair itself; waiting for full historical disclosure and accuracy regarding the prodigious global effort, which occurred a century and more ago, to create the present State of Israel.

The answer to the question pertaining to the manner, tactics and strategy by which, Weizmann was able to accomplish the ends of his purpose to quickly effect the dislodging of Brandeis, is provided in two books – one, which we have already referenced; "A History of Zionism" (Laqueur:1972), and curiously, "Albert Einstein in America, 1921" (Walter Isaacson:2000)(see also, by the same author "Einstein : His life and Universe"(2007).

First to Laqueur, who informs us "Balfour (the British Foreign Secretary) met Brandeis twice during his visit to Washington in April, 1917, and American Jewry 's interest in Palestine, was impressed on him". Nonetheless, much to Weizmann's chagrin, when Balfour, requested from the American President a statement of sympathy – Wilson demurred (based on the U.S. State Department's contrary advice) . . . However, "By mid-October (Sir William) Wiseman, head of British intelligence in the United States (and a partner in Jacob Schiff's investment firm – Kuhn Loeb); had informed the (British) Foreign Office that Wilson (subject to the changes as recommended by Brandeis), approved the formula decided upon by the British War Cabinet. The Zionists had surmounted yet another major hurdle owing to the help received from American Jewry".

The battleground regarding the impending Balfour Declaration now shifted from Washington to London. It was no easy or simple thing for Weizmann, to achieve consensus among the British Zionists relative to their conflicting positions – if, in the event, the British War Cabinet made a definitive public statement relating to the future of Palestine. In any event, Weizmann was waiting outside the cabinet rooms, when Sir Mark Sykes of the Foreign Office, burst forth from the chamber and approached Weizmann, enthusiastically saying – "it's a boy". As Weizmann later noted "I did not like the boy". And, even though, the Declaration's content was somewhat watered down: Weizmann fully realized the overwhelming meaning and significance of the Declaration (in the form of a letter from the British cabinet to Lord Walter Rothschild) respecting and affecting, not only every aspect of Zionism, and every Jew – whether Zionist or not – but as well, the entire post Great War world.

In order for Weizmann to triumph in his search to manifest a unified world Zionism under his exclusive leadership, it would be necessary at the very least, to neutralize any opposition and purge any potential rival to his leadership—no matter their national origin. In that respect, it is important to realize that Weizmann was an early Anglophile. And, although, he received his scientific education in Germany and Switzerland, Weizmann happily became a naturalized British subject, who lived and worked in Manchester as a bio-chemist. Beyond that, he was an ardent patriot, who after inventing (by the use of horse chestnuts) artificial acetone (essential to the British war effort and the production of cordite to provide smokeless artillery shells); generously, contributed the patent to the government.

As did every other Jew, Weizmann despised the Russians, but did not necessarily trust the Germans. However, his innate perspicacity persuaded him that the Americans and their highly popular and respected leader – Louis Brandeis, were essential to his plans—both during the remainder of the War and after its immediate aftermath. Weizmann unmistakably knew that in order to succeed with his plan for the incipient Jewish nation to achieve Dominion status within the British Empire; Brandeis somehow, subsequent to the War's end – had to be ejected from both the American and world Zionist movements. For no American— least of all – Brandeis, and his American colleagues, would agree to such an obvious Anglophile composition of the future state.

There was, nonetheless, a very large and glaring flaw to be solved. A meeting of the American Zionist Organization had been scheduled for June, 1921 to take place in Cleveland, Ohio. That city, of course, was located in the United States. A nation, which knew very little of Weizmann. That undeniable fact included the Jewish-American Zionists, whose representatives would be attending the meeting.

The identity problem was solved – by none other than the newly famous Dr. Albert Einstein [2]. For an explanation of this strange turning of the hinge of fate, we must visit Walter Isaacson's "Albert Einstein in America 1921". The full exposition of this unusual Einstein aspect.

commences however, a year earlier in London: concise particulars of which, are related by Laqueur in his "History of Zionism"

"The 1920 London (Zionist) conference was not fully representative of the federations and trends, which composed the world movement. The right-wing and religious parties were much more represented than the left. American and German Zionists had only relatively small delegations. Since it was the first major Zionist meeting for seven years, it became almost automatically the battleground between the main contenders for leadership. American Zionists under "Brandeis and the (non-German) Europeans under Weizmann.

As far as Brandeis was concerned, it was not a contest for personal power, for, as a Supreme Court Justice of the United States, he was unwilling to accept any position other than that of Honorary President.

"It was a clash between two different concepts regarding the future of the Zionist movement, but there were also discernible differences in style and approach. The slogan of 'Washington against Pinsk', under which the battle was waged was a distortion of a highly complex situation, but there certainly was more than a mere a grain of truth in it. The American Zionists, who had carried the major financial burden from the beginning of the War, and who had played a central part in the political struggle before and after the Balfour Declaration, were extremely critical of the political leadership in London in which, they were unrepresented. Brandeis believed correctly, "that with the Balfour Declaration, or at the very latest with "(the Jewish) Lord Samuel's appointment as British High Commissioner to the Mandate, the main political task of the Movement had been accomplished, and that from that epic moment every energy had to be devoted to the building of Palestine.

"The American Zionists opposed the establishment of a big executive office in London, feeling that the work for Palestine had to be done in Jerusalem. They favored decentralization and the introduction of modern business methods. American Jews it was claimed had greater administrative expertise than their European brethren".

Moreover, the Americans did not align with European Socialist colonization methods, and favored capitalism, free enterprise, American style 'know how', combined with their innate 'Yankee' sense of initiative and excellence." They were willing to exert themselves on behalf of the Zionist cause, but they demanded that their contribution should be directed only to Palestinian projects. They found it scandalous that the rich Jews of Europe, of whom there were many, were unwilling to take upon themselves a similar burden and thought that that the (proposed) tithing of wealthy Jews was unrealistic. They wanted a clear division between commercial investments in Palestine and voluntary donations. They were not in favor of Diaspora nationalism, and refused to pay for Zionist activities outside of Palestine" As well, they wanted immediate large scale Eastern European immigration, for settlement on the Jewish 'Homeland' Palestinian territories. Before Great Britain – in the vagaries of its own indigenous politics, had a change of heart or mind – or both.

Above all, "Brandeis was put off by Weizmann's behavior; having reached agreement with him, Weizmann had acted behind his back, to torpedo their accord. He was irritated by the proceedings at the London conference, the lack of preparation, order and purpose; absence of any real authority, the constant speech-making. Brandeis, in brief, did not like what he saw of world Zionism.

"Weizmann and the Europeans branded Brandeis policy as 'Zionism without Zion'. The American Zionists lacked a 'Jewish heart'.

"They had never understood the basic character of political Zionism or the demand for a revolution in Jewish life. Instead, they proposed an ersatz Zionism. The Weizmann Europeans argued that Palestine could not be colonized in the same way as America had been built – by private enterprise – but that a central national effort was required. Criteria of efficiency and business management were not the only ones, applicable to a Movement idealistic in character. This referred, inter alia to the American opposition to collective agricultural settlements, which they predicted would only cause further deficits in the Zionist budget."

The struggle to control the Zionist movement, and the seeds of the victory of the British-led European Zionists over Brandeis and the Americans, had been strewn more than a decade earlier; and, rested upon the vision and efforts of three remarkable men. Those individuals portrayed a striking example of whenever the hinge of fate turns – it produces extraordinary results. In this case, that hinge was a vibrant, growing British city – a commercial and industrial center – which was home to a large Jewish population. That city was Manchester, and in its British dynamic mercantilism, the paths of three outstanding men crossed: Winston Churchill, David Lloyd George and Chaim Weizmann. Two of whom, were to become Prime Ministers of Great Britain and one, the first President of the State of Israel.

David Lloyd George—Prime Minister of Great Britain from 1916 to 1922 – was a Manchester born Welshman, who was raised an Evangelical Christian. His first language was not English, but Welsh. Nonetheless, he wrote, spoke and articulated elegantly, in either one. While several of Britain's Prime Ministers have been Barristers, Lloyd George was the only one who was a Solicitor. In matters of religion he was not only an evangelist, but a fervent non-conformist who successfully led the fight to disestablish the Anglican Church in Wales. He was first elected to Parliament in 1890, and made Chancellor of the Exchequer in 1911. He was of advanced social views, and the first to introduce health and employment benefits to the British public. He was also an unabashed womanizer, fiery orator, and rival of Churchill for the future leadership of the Liberal party.

C.P. Scott the Editor of the Manchester Guardian had met Weizmann at a garden party and, impressed by the engaging Weizmann persona, shortly thereafter arranged a meeting for him with Lloyd George. They found that they had much in common: Lloyd George's fundamentalist Christian beliefs and opinions concurring quite perfectly, with those of the Zionist leader. It was the once and future governor of Palestine – Herbert (Lord) Samuel, who as early as December, 1914, carried the message to Weizmann that the Asquith Liberal administration favored the establishment of a Jewish Homeland.

The dye was cast, but not yet completely set to permit the hinge to turn. For such an event, an additional person was required. That person (immediately before and after, he "re-ratted" (i.e., changed his political allegiance for a second time), was the extraordinary Tory politician, journalist, soldier and famed writer – Winston Leonard

Spencer Churchill; who at the time, fortuitously was the sitting member for Manchester: a constituency comprised of one third Jewish voters.

On December, 10, 1905, Churchill addressed a meeting in his Manchester Riding, which was held to protest the latest of several outrageous Russian Pogroms. The late Sir Martin Gilbert – the official biographer of Churchill – in "Churchill and the Jews "(2007), notes:

"Among those present on the platform when Churchill spoke was a brilliant Jewish chemist and active Zionist, Russian born and naturalized British subject, Dr. Chaim Weizmann, who had come from Geneva, where he was a lecturer in chemistry to a professorship at the University of Manchester. The two men, who were born three days apart, were to become closely associated in the evolution of Zionist needs and policies."

The son of a small but successful, timber merchant, Weizmann was educated in Berlin and Switzerland. Virtually unknown anywhere before 1914, he "came to dominate Zionism as no other person had since Herzl". It was into this profound Anglo-centric milieu that Brandeis and the American Zionists unwittingly, perhaps – even naïvely, stepped.

How then, as has been previously posed, was the completely unknown foreigner – Weizmann – able to become so popularized within the American Zionist movement, that eventually he could vanquish the formidable Brandeis for domination of world Zionism? The answer resided in but one man – perhaps, the greatest genius and creative thinker known to the twentieth century – Dr. Albert Einstein.

THE EINSTEIN FACTOR

Walter Isaacson in "Albert Einstein in America, 1921" explains:

"Albert Einstein's growing fame and budding Zionism came together in the spring of 1921 for an event that was unique in the history of science, and indeed remarkable for any realm: a grand two-month processional through the eastern and mid-western United States that evoked the kind of mass frenzy and adulation that would thrill a touring rock star. The world had never seen before, and perhaps never will again, such a celebrated scientific superstar, one who also happened to be a gentle icon of humanist values, and a living patron saint for Jews. [2]

"Einstein had initially thought that his first visit to America might be a way to make some money in a stable currency in order to provide for his family in Switzerland. 'I have demanded $15,000 from Princeton and Wisconsin', he wrote his friend and fellow scientist Paul Ehrenfest it will probably scare them off. But, if they do bite, I will be buying economic independence for myself – and, that's not a thing to sniff at"

In fact, the American Universities did not bite "My demands are too high", Einstein reported to Ehrenfest. Thus, by February, 1921, he had made other plans for the Spring. He would present a paper at the third Solway Conference in Brussels, and give some lectures in London at the behest of Ehrenfest.

"It was then that Karl Blumenfeld, leader of the German Zionist, came by Einstein's apartment with an invitation in the form of a telegram, from the President of the World Zionist Organization, Chaim Weizmann. Weizmann's telegram invited Einstein to accompany him on a trip to America, to raise funds to help settle Palestine and, in particular, to help create the Hebrew University in Jerusalem. When Blumenthal read it to him, Einstein primarily balked. He was not an orator, he said. And, the role of simply using his celebrity to draw crowds to the cause was 'an unworthy one'. Blumenthal remonstrated, saying to Einstein that if he considered himself a Zionist – and took his conversion to the cause seriously – then, he must go to America with Weizmann. To the boundless astonishment of Blumenthal, Einstein then stated 'I realize that I am now part of the situation, and that I must accept the invitation.'

And, so it came to pass that on March, 21, 1921, Einstein accompanied by Weizmann, sailed from the Netherlands. What took place thereafter was the crystallization of Weizmann's plan, whereby his name and face would be easily recognizable throughout the major cities of America. Einstein's every movement was closely shadowed by Weizmann and where Einstein went – so did Chaim Weizmann.

Einstein was lionized by the American public: he was the first of the celebrity age icon personalities, and his picture was published countless times in newspapers across the United States. In many of those photos the smiling countenance of the always charming Weizmann appears. For, in fact and deed, by the time of their ship's docking in New York, Chaim Weizmann had become Einstein's friend, fellow scientist and mutually zealous Zionist colleague.

It was a brilliant plan expertly executed. Weizmann was now in the minds of America, closely associated with Einstein, his face and commentary – known and familiar to hundreds of thousands of Jews – including: those who would be attending the convention of the American Zionist Organization, to be held in Cleveland during the third week in June, 1921.

It is thus not surprising that "Einstein was treated warily by American Jewish leaders, such as Louis Brandeis": And, with very good reason for the forthcoming Cleveland Convention, and their eventual fate as luminaries of the Zionist movement, cast a looming shadow.

The struggle for the control and leadership of the American Zionist organization ultimately ended with the defeat of Brandeis and his colleagues at the Cleveland Convention. "Brandeis resigned as Honorary President and together with his leading supporters, Felix Frankfurter, Rabbi Stephen Wise, Nathan Strauss, Abba Hillel Silver, and Julian Mack withdrew from active work in the organization. And, while several of his colleagues in time returned, for Brandeis the decision was final."

A schism had occurred that was to continue until the international crises of the mid-nineteen thirties. "For the East Europeans—Zionism was their whole life; for Brandeis (and his colleagues in the American Zionist movement), it was just one of several pre-occupations, albeit an important one. For this reason, if no other, the Brandeis faction was bound to lose the struggle for the character and future policy of the Movement." By the time of the 1947 U.N. Resolution 181, regarding the Partition of Palestine, there remained only a vestigial sliver of land, to become the long-awaited State of Israel. In other words, Weizmann's genuine aspirations for an Anglophile Jewish Homeland, as part of the British Commonwealth and Empire, were betrayed, if not totally crushed, by the very same nation that had given him and world Zionism, the Balfour Declaration.

Concurrent, with those events, the Second World War intervened: the catastrophic Holocaust occurred, yet the split within Zionism – perhaps, for very different political reasons and under varied persons, philosophies and cultures, endured — until May, 14, 1948. After that date, for every Jew, no matter their prior view, opinion or belief – there was only one cause – the cause for the continued existence, preservation and flowering of the State of Israel.

NOTES

(1) My book "Enemies and Allies: Seven Days of Destiny" (Second Printing,2013), attempted to briefly portray not only the remarkable, complicated, but brilliant man, behind the birth of the "Dream", but as well the 1895 Viennese political, social and cultural milieu in which, Herzl and his Austro-Hungarian co-religionist of like mind, thrived.

(2) It should be remembered that in a 1921 eclipse of the sun, photographed on a mountain top on the West African island of Principe, the British Astronomer Sir Arthur Eddington at great personal risk, indisputably proved the theories of the obscure German Astro-Physicist Albert Einstein to be unmistakably correct. From that moment onward, Newton's age-old view that it was gravity and gravity alone, which held together the cosmos – were destroyed. As a result, Einstein's fame instantly spread across not only the scientific world, but in popular imagination – immeasurably resulting in the creation of our contemporary society.

SOURCES

The sources relied upon in the foregoing were many, among them are:

The Complete Diaries of Theodore Herzl: Herzl Foundation (1960)

Churchill and the Jews: Sir Martin Gilbert (2007)

Mostly Morgenthaus: Henry Morgenthau III (1991)

The Pity of It All: Amos Elon (2002)

A Controversy of Zion: Geoffrey Wheatcroft (1996)

A Peace to end all Peace: David Fromkin (1996)

A History of Zionism: Walter Lacquer (1972)

Jerusalem: The Biography: Montefiore Sebag (2011)

Brandeis: Lewis J Paper (1983)

A GALLERY OF PERSONS INVOLVED

Albert Einstein

"A living patron saint of all Jews"

Louis Brandeis

Zionism's Almost Forgotten Hero

"He saw himself as a better American because
he wanted a homeland for his people".

David Lloyd George

A fiery orator, womanizer and rival of Churchill;
"His fundamentalist Christian opinions and beliefs
coincided perfectly with Weizmann's Zionism"

"The idea behind your movement is a healthy one" Kaiser
Wilhelm II to Herzl: Jerusalem, November 2, 1898

Winston Churchill

"With true comradeship, there will be room enough for all."

Theodore Herzl

In less than 50 years his dream became political reality.

Chaim Weizmann

The first President of the State of Israel. He came to dominate
Zionism as no other person since Herzl.

President Woodrow Wilson

"Anything you can do will reflect upon America. You may count on the full power of this Administration to back you up". Wilson to Henry Morgenthau;

Henry Morgenthau Sr.

"Constantinople is the point at which the interests of American Jews and the welfare of Jews in Palestine are focused; it is indisputable that I have a Jew at that post" Wilson to Morgenthau.

IMAGE SOURCES

https://www.google.com/url?sa=i&url=https%3A%2F%2Fen.
mogaznews.com%2FWorld-News%2F655643%2FHow-the-young-
Winston-Churchill-was-flayed-alive.html&psig=AOvVaw3Re7R2Cl
07hB8SODWaAN25&ust=1588955547138000&source=images&cd
=vfe&ved=0CA0QjhxqFwoTCJj04_CWoukCFQAAAAAdAAAAA
BBp

https://pixabay.com/photos/albert-einstein-1921-portrait-1145030/

https://commons.wikimedia.org/w/index.php?search=woodrow+
wilson&title=Special%3ASearch&go=Go&ns0=1&ns6=1&ns12=1
&ns14=1&ns100=1&ns106=1#/media/File:Woodrow_Wilson_(1912).jpg

https://commons.wikimedia.org/w/index.php?search=david+lloyd+
george&title=Special:Search&go=Go&ns0=1&ns6=1&ns12=1&ns14
=1&ns100=1&ns106=1&searchToken=2clx2jejpgtb7k4jv0t4m443
b#%2Fmedia%2FFile%3ALloydGeorge_%28cropped%29.jpg

https://commons.wikimedia.org/w/index.php?search=Theodore
+Herzl&title=Special:Search&go=Go&ns0=1&ns6=1&ns12
=1&ns14=1&ns100=1&ns106=1&searchToken=bwf6i8vnjkt26r0
wecyry9xry#%2Fmedia%2FFile%3ATheodore_Herzl.jpg

https://commons.wikimedia.org/w/index.php?search=Wilhelm+the+2nd&title=Special:Search&go=Go&ns0=1&ns6=1&ns12=1&ns14=1&ns100=1&ns106=1&searchToken=dqs8yd1nccvnux2xgjvqje8y9#%2Fmedia%2FFile%3APikiWiki_Israel_28529_Herzl_with_Caesar_Wilhelm_the_2nd.jpg

https://en.wikipedia.org/wiki/Louis_Brandeis#/media/File:Brandeisl.jpg

https://www.google.com/url?sa=i&url=https%3A%2F%2Fwww.wikiwand.com%2Fen%2FHenry_Morgenthau_Sr &psig=AOvVaw2Bx55buUSB6CvVQTVh9Md5&ust1588955439633000&source=images&cd=vfe&ved=0CA0QjhxqFwoTCKiGqbeWoukCFQAAAAAdAAAAABAD

www.ingramcontent.com/pod-product-compliance
Lightning Source LLC
Chambersburg PA
CBHW031428250726
48656CB00002B/892